I Am The Crocus

I Am The Crocus

Poems by Children from County Wicklow

Edited by David Wheatley

I Am The Crocus

Poems by Children from County Wicklow

Edited by David Wheatley

First published in 1998 © Wicklow County Council
Produced by Wicklow County Council

ISBN 0-9533904-2-X

The Arts Council
An Chomhairle Ealaíon

Wicklow County Council wishes to acknowledge assistance provided by Wicklow Rural Partnership Ltd. for this publication.

I am delighted to introduce this this anthology, the subject matter of which has been provided by the many students of our national schools who participated in the 1998 Wicklow County Council Writer in Residence programme. I acknowledge the difficult editorial task that was David Wheatley's, our Writer in Residence to the county this year, and join with him in his acknowledgement of the continuing tradition and superb quality of the work of our young writers across the county.

Blaise Treacy

Blaise Treacy
County Manager, Wicklow County Council.

On behalf of the members of Wicklow County Council I am delighted to acknowledge this delightful selection of poetry by our young writers in County Wicklow. I also wish to acknowledge the work of the arts section and the county library service. I would like to congratulate David Wheatley on this volume and wish him the very best with his writing in the future. I know that this selection will be enjoyed by our population young and old as well as our many visitors to the county.

Liam Kavanagh

Cllr. Liam Kavanagh
Chairman, Wicklow County Council.

Children do lots of useful things in school. They learn writing and sums, they play football and hurling, they have concerts and go on school trips. But deep down every child knows what the most important thing about school is: writing poems. Up and down the county, from Shillelagh to Bray and Arklow to Blessington, there are hundreds and hundreds of children writing exuberant, witty and marvellous poetry. *I Am The Crocus* is my selection of their work.

Children in Wicklow take their writing very seriously. I remember meeting a young man in Shillelagh who wanted to read me a poem, but went so fast he kept having to stop. His teacher told him to try slowing down, to which he replied 'I have to go that fast or else it doesn't rhyme!' And rhyme is *very* important, as we all know.

Often on my visits to schools, when I'd read my poems and the children read theirs, we'd end up writing new ones together on the blackboard. Here's one that sticks in my memory from Glenealy, discussing the serious business of who'd make the England eleven in the World Cup. It's a special sort of poem that the Japanese call a haiku:

Gazza got left out.
He ate too many kebabs.
Owen's much better.

Here's another, from Baltinglass, that spells out 'Wicklow' with the first letter of each line:

Wet and windy
Is Wicklow
Cold and chilly
Kingdom of mountains
Lakes and rivers
Only place for me
Wonderful Wickow!

It was a cold and rainy day when we wrote it, but as you can see, our affection for the place came through in the end.

The only sad thing about this book is that there wasn't space for everyone's work. To anyone who was left out I say: don't be too disappointed. Writers in residence are a bit like buses—another one is bound to be along soon, and another anthology too. And to all the young writers who did make it in I'd like to say: make sure you keep writing, and may this be only the first of many books you appear in!

David Wheatley
September 1998

Mother

My Mother is the kindest person on the earth,
She brings me everywhere I want to go.

My Mother is the sweetest woman on the planet,
If I want anything she gives it to me.

My Mother gives me money even if I don't want it,
My Mother buys me the toys I want,
I love my Mammy so much I want to hug her right now.

Zoe Elliott

My Mother

My Mother does the shopping and cleaning and all,
She always talks on the telephone.

She can sew and knit,
It's so great to have her around.

Some Mothers are fussy, my Mother's not,
She has black short curly hair.

My Mother likes dainty things,
She is not fussy, she is so clean.

She is my Mother,
She is the best.

I love her and no one else,
She is my Mother and I am proud
to have her around,
I am really, really, so, so proud.

Edel Ferguson

Teletubbies

Tubbies, Tubbies are so funny,
They have tellies in their tummies,
They are funny, cuddly, cute and kind.

All four are nice,
I don't mind that Tubby custard is what they love,
I myself don't call that grub,
Pink and gooey, it's so funny,
People who made them make lots of money.

I think they're cooler than school,
I think Teletubbies rule.

Anne Marie Byrne

I Don't Want to Go to School!

Mom oh Mom I feel sick,
My head hurts, it feels like a brick.

Teacher will be there tomorrow,
She won't believe my tale of sorrow.

Mother Mother what shall I do,
Please give me a little clue.

My coat is on,
I'm ready to go with a disprin down
my throat you know.

Mother wouldn't believe my lie,
With a pat on the head she waved goodbye.

Aine Murphy

When Daddy Cooked Dinner

When Daddy cooked dinner it was quite a disaster,
The potatoes were so disgusting it was like eating plaster.

The turnips were brown and the peas rock hard
and the carrots could have been mistaken for corrugated card.

Daddy made a good attempt at cooking dinner,
but in the end he had to part with a tenner
as take-aways aren't free.

Stephanie Connolly

The Farm

The fields are soggy and wet,
When the animals are ill I go to the vet,
I'm happy, I'm glad,
I'm miserable and sad,
That is the life on the farm.

Kevin Hipwell

The Mouse

There once was a mouse,
Who lived in a house down the hillside road,
This little mouse went from house to house,
Eating all the cheese.

Kevin Hipwell

The Lucky Find

There was a young boy from down the road,
who found a twenty pound note on the ground,
He thought for a while,
And said with a smile,
I think I'll bring it to the Lost and Found.

Kenneth Greene

The Crane

Lift up heavy metal,
Pouring down like a hot kettle,
Lifting up unwanted rubbish,
Picking up and throwing away.

I'm all alone in a pile of rubbish,
I wish someone would visit me,
I wanted to be a boat in a quay,
I'm very old and very rusty.

Here I am all brave and tall,
Everything below me feels so small,
I'm very used to all the cars,
I pick them up like chocolate bars.

I see the same things every day,
I wish I was a heap that lay,
I wanted to be shiny and brand new,
A bit of excitement everyday too.

But here I'll lay,
And I'll lay here too,
And I'll always want something brand new,
But I'll always know it won't come true.

I have an arm that's called a hook,
I'm very nosy to have a look,
I'm very lonely and very sad,
But some day I can be assured to be glad.

For even though everything around me feels so small,
Some day I'll be proud to call myself tall.

Shane Keenan

Trees and Leaves

Up in the trees are leaves I see,
Brown and red as they fall on my head,
And I play in the leaves for all the day,
except for evening when they get swept away.

Martina O'Regan

Rules

It isn't fair,
All these stupid rules,
Don't comb your hair,
Don't act like fools.

Sit in your place,
Don't stand on the soil,
Don't make a face,
Treat us like royal.

Don't wear high heels,
Don't fight at all,
Keep away from the fields,
Don't bring a ball.

If I was in charge,
I'd shut the school,
Float on a barge,
And look really cool.

Cliodhna Denny

In the Summer

In the summer time it's nice and hot,
Get your bucket and spade and come with the lot.

Don't forget your sun cream
because there is a sun beam.

If you're lucky the sun will shine all day round
and the little birds singing have a lovely sound.

Children play down by the bay,
They swim and splash in the sea all day.

Children running around in their togs,
Some of them are playing with their dogs.

Summer time is so fun,
With the lovely bright shining sun.

Emma Willis and Sasha Farrell

Untitled

Jennifer Williams,
Sticky fingers,
Stand up straight in line.

Sam Clark,
I'm deducting a mark,
For bringing a mangy feline.

Suzie Best,
Give it a rest,
I've already told you once.

Jamie Mayor,
Stop pulling her hair,
Don't fall oh you clutz.

Thank God school's over,
I've lost my pullover,
Oh where's that child gone.

I told you to wait here,
Because you were late dear,
Now stay still and I won't be long.

Aisling Carey

The Homeless Man

As he stands by the shop window,
Everyone can hear him cry,
Food or money, please have mercy,
But everyone walks by.

In the night he's in the shelter,
Built for homeless men,
But once the dawn breaks,
He's on the streets again.

Nobody bothers about a man without money,
Children laugh at him,
They think his life is funny.

Put yourself in that poor man's shoes,
Imagine in his hear,
the ever lasting bruise.

Knowing he will never be loved or cared about,
What do you think of the poor man now.

Grace O'Connor

Cars Are

Fumeful beasts,
All colours to be seen,
Polluting the air,
Driving through cities,
Repairs need to be done,
Rattling along main roads,
Shooting fumes into the air,
On to the garage for repairs.

Owen Plant

When I Get Angry

When I get angry,
I start punching!
and stamping!
roaring!
and screaming!
Whacking!
and exploding!
destroying!
and killing!
and then I settle down.

Cormac Lennon

Monsters are...

Terrifying beasts
Crazy destroyers
Enormous predators
America's most wanted
Indestructible killers
Dangerous
Easy to spot, but difficult to get away from,
Never friendly.

Aengus Walton

16 to Go

To see 16 people go
Is not very nice you know.
To see them go so young
Just as they were having fun.

Some best friends side by side
They all just simply died.
To see the bullets just fly and fly
It's silly to see young children die.

Just as they were having fun.
A man bursts in with a gun.
Bang, bang, bye, bye.
Don't let their parents cry.

Alan Dutton

Death

Death is the colour of black,
A dreadful thing,
Sadness and crying,
Upset and horrified.

Ruth McKeown

Dogs

Dogs are very playful,
Dogs are sometimes vicious,
Dogs are sometimes friendly,
Dogs are very cute,
Dogs are very fast,
Dogs are very hairy,
Dogs are very smart,
Dogs have very sharp teeth.

Jonathan Chadwick

Snow

It was snowing outside,
So very cold,
The snowflakes were spinning,
So brass and bold.

I'm tucked away,
In my warm bed,
The snow is swirling around,
But not a word it says.

Eva Coller

Battle

English soldiers around the cottage,
McAllister at the door.

Shouts saying 'you go on!',
Bullets flying by.

Blood on the ground,
Escape in the outlaws minds.

One bullet heads straight for him,
Now death is in the air.

Aoife Lennon

Anger

Anger is red,
It tastes like very hot curry.

Anger smells like boiling bubbling water,
It looks like trees on fire.

It sounds like drums banging,
Anger feels like wrecking the house.

Eva Coller

A Cat

I know a cat who is black,
And always ready to attack,
She is small,
And very tall,
So that's all.

Edwina Hanbidge

Nature

The light wind blows,
It makes me shiver,
The calm river flows,
I walk gently on my feet,
To hear the birds so sweet,
I freeze to ice,
To hear nature so nice.

Aisling Murray

My Hobby

My hobby is to sing,
It is a wonderful thing,
To hear the sound of ring a ding ding,
My hobby is to sing.

My hobby is to run,
It is a lot of fun,
I like to run in the sun,
My hobby is to run.

My hobby is to climb,
I also like to rhyme,
I think that it is time,
To end this rhyme of mine.

Aisling Murray

Why I Was Late for School

Teacher, dear teacher,
You won't believe what happened to me!
On my way down to school I bumped into a tree,
The I saw a horse,
A big one of course,
Come galloping towards me,
I closed my eyes and covered my head,
But what luck, it stopped and dropped dead,
As I climbed to my feet my head in a jumble,
I walked down the street and took a wrong turn,
And guess what?
I ended up in a jungle!
Then suddenly a lion came up and ate me,
And he spat me out in the sea,
I got stuck on an island for hours,
But I picked you some nice flowers,
And that's why I'm late for school.

Katie Evans

When I am Frightened

When I am frightened,
I screech, scream and roar,
I call for my Daddy,
And I run out the door.

My Daddy comes in
and puts me to bed,
There's still shadows and ghosts,
Going around in my head.

I stay close to the wall,
With my back to the door,
I'm falling asleep,
I'm not scared anymore.

Laurie Ahern

Bedtime

Everything is so cosy,
Because I am so rosy,
Mummy tucked me in,
Now my sleep begins,
Dreaming of little people in my head,
But I won't let them in my bed.

Leanne Harte

The Blitz

There had been severe bombing the previous night,
And as we were putting up the blackouts,
Everyone was silent,
But were all thinking the same thing.

That night up in bed,
Thinking of the danger ahead,
I got under the covers,
I had left my ordinary clothes on.

As I was just relaxing, there came a siren,
Then another and another,
My body felt frozen,
Everybody was screaming,
I pulled myself out of bed,
And grabbed my baby sister,
But she was dead.

I ran out of the house,
To the air-raid shelter,
All I could hear was
The crash and the bang,
A warden walked over,
And a chill came over my body,
He touched me on the shoulder,
And said my family was dead.

Eimear Ryan

The Wedding Day

A very special day has come,
If he decides not to run,
I put my hair up in a bun,
and put my garter on for fun.

I take my dress out from the press,
and dance around thinking I'm the best,
As I went to say goodbye,
The only thing I could do was cry.

The car is waiting outside the gate,
So I must hurry before I'm late.
I pick my flowers up from the chair,
And everyone said, 'God bless, take care.'

Then I got in the big black car,
But I didn't have to go that far,
As the car began to roar,
I paused to think what lay in store.

As we walked slowly up the aisle,
There were tears in my eyes,
But my face wore a smile,
My Dad gave the groom my hand,
And the Priest beckoned us all to stand.

As everything was silent and still,
We repeated after the Priest, 'I will',
We both made our vows to be loyal and true,
To love one another our whole life through.

Zena Archer

The World

If we kill our World,
We kill ourselves too.
If we have poisonous gases in our World,
We have poisonous gases in us too.
If we have nuclear power plants in our World,
We have radiation in us too.
If we have smoke in our World,
We have smoke in us too.
If there is pollution in our water,
We have pollution in us too.

but ....

If we don't use fumes,
Our air will be fresh.
If we recycled,
we would not waste our natural resources.
If we had no pollution,
Our Earth would be clean.
If we had no nuclear power plants,
Our air would be fresh.
If we had no smoke,
Our lungs would be healthy.
If we looked after our World,
Our World would look after us.

Chloe Kinsella

The Prayer of the Crocus

Dear Lord,

I am the crocus,
all I ask is to keep me safe and
tell the children not to step on me.

Thank you for giving me life
and after that for keeping me safe
when I was just a little bulb.

Amen

Emily Leonard

Bad Weather

Rain is like a tear,
Covered by clouds that look
like big marshmallows.

The clouds are turning black as coal,
then there is thunder,
It is as loud as a bomb going off.

The ground shakes like an Earthquake,
Then suddenly there's a light in the sky,
it is lightning.

Sarah Flynn

Night in the Woods

I was surrounded with black
And the moonlit sky.
I heard strange noises,
As I walked by.

It was like a black room
with a whole of light.
It was the moon,
It was a lovely sight.

It was pretty frightening,
As the tree crouched round.
There was also lightning,
That crashed to the ground.

I will always remember,
That night in the wood.
All the things I saw, heard,
As I just stood.

Sarah Ryan

My Dogs

One Sunday afternoon at the end of May,
I got a beautiful puppy for my eighth birthday.
I called her Holly, she was such a dote,
Soft and silky was her golden coat.

Some time later when she had matured,
She had nine little puppies that everyone adored.
Eight went to homes, they were a sight to behold,
We kept 'Lady' who's extremely bold.

We go for long walks to the woods and the beach,
and my dogs run to places that I can't reach.
When I whistle or call them they come running to me,
and their favourite place is a swim in the sea.

They're my two best friends from the moment they came,
Without them my life would never be the same.

Paula Byrne

Alliteration

Windy Wandy wobbled weirdly,
Timmy Tommy toddler toddled down the toilet.
Teenage Tina threw Terry Timble
Filthy Froggy flicked the fork
Fishy Fred fought fat fish fingers
Single Sue sat sulking on a sofa
Snakes sliddered slyly sniffing the smelly squid
Elephants eat eclairs after eight
Nelly Napkin knotted napkins
Tiny Tammy tickled the Teletubbies

Donna Campbell

Alliteration

One waddling, webbed water duck
Waded and wailed while watching whirlpools.

Two tiny tots tormented teachers terribly,
Three thoughtless thickos thought about three thrushes.

Four freaky fat frogs freaked out
Four fat foxes fought them furiously on the floor.
Five fast Ferraris were fined fifty French francs.

Six strange psychos stared slyly at sizzling sausages
Seven smiling slugs slithered sneakily past seven sly snails.

Eight enormous elephants ate eggs excitedly and eternally.
Nine nifty knees knocked against nurse Nancy's nice knees
knocking them about.
Ten teachers told tales, ten teenagers are tattle-tails.

Rachel Breen

Animals

A horse galloped through a field
Like wind on a stormy night
The sheep all disappeared into their huts,
Like clouds disappearing for the sunlight.

The pigs all tossed and turned in the mud,
Like sizzling sausages turning in a pan.

And all the pigs were brown and muddy,
Like a person with a tan.

Julie Traynor

Spring

Spring is the time for flowers
Tulips, daffodils and bluebells
They all come in April showers
And bring their own spring smells

Spring is daffodil yellow
It's clover green
There's an old blue fellow
Called Pussy Willow Screen
He roams the land in spring
Making things nice for him
But as well as Pussy Willow
There's Catkins Pillow
Who spreads the wings
On chicks and birds to make them
Fly and sing
Across the sky.

Teddy O'Donoghue

I Like Noise

The crash of giant waves crashing on enormous rocks.
The thud of a fisherman's boat coming ashore.
The roar of trucks with lots of buckskin in back.
The screech of car tyres skidding round sharp bends.
The rumble of rocks avalanching through the sloping trees.
The sweet sound of the tattoo of the drummer's drum.
The sweet pitter patter of the raindrops on my window.
The hoist of the mind blowing all the autumn leaves away.
I LIKE NOISE!!

Philip Dudley

Wild Cat

Gleaming green eyes
Stare around
Whiskers twitching
Crouching down low
Tail waving, ready waiting
For the prey!

The noise of small feet
Scampering across the wooden floor
It stops
Looks and then continues
It didn't see the dark shadow
Crouching down, ready, waiting
The small feet scampered on.

Suddenly there's a squeak
Then a scream
And a loud meow
A few minutes later the cat came out
Licking its chops
Looking very pleased with itself.

Linley Brownrigg

The Calf is Born

The stolid cow lay there
In the draughty old shed
Waiting to give birth to her calf
She lay there sweating and panting

The other cows watched her
Wondering what would happen
The farmer watched her
Saying 'You can do it girl!'

Suddenly a head appeared
Then the body
The calf was there
The cow licked it and everyone rejoiced.

Sandra Stephenson

Noise

Foot steps walking across the landing
Lurking on its way
The wardrobe creaks
The hanging aeroplane starts up

It turns into an eagle
It claws and crows and
Claws some more.
The car starts up its engine
It revs across my feet.
I go up my courage and fall
Out of bed.

To my amazement
I saw my first friend
Muzzy my imaginary friend
Now I'm tucked up in bed
safe from the world
Now I can sleep.

Shane Marah

The Flood

The warmth of the fire,
The entertainment of the television,
The door opens,
'Come quick, come quick!' he shouts,
We grab our coats and boots,
Confused.

We run out the door,
The winds slowing us down,
Then to our surprise,
The drive,
The sheds,
All flooded.

'Quick get the dog,
Round up the sheep,'
Across the road I run,
To open the gate.

All goes well,
The sheep are safe,
And I'm tucked in bed,
Asleep and safe.

Ellen Fox

Untitled

When I move to my new house,
will I like the street
Will I like the school there
What sort of people will I meet

Will there be nice teachers in the school
Or will they be strict and make us obey
all the rules when I start
Or will it be easy
Will it have computers
Art
Knitting or singing

Will my road be big or small
Will the children be tiny or tall
Will I enjoy playing with them all
Playing races or even basketball

Will this place make us change
Or will we still be the same
Will I see my old friends again
I wonder, I wonder, in my new home.

Kerry Gallagher

After We've Gone

What will everything be like
When I have gone away?
Will there still be protection
from the ozone layer?

Will there be pollution
going into the sea?
With all the people swimming in it,,
I'm glad it won't be me.

What if people go to the moon
or under the sea?
Because the earth might be crowded,
I'm glad it won't be me.

Will there still be wild animals
roaring in Africa?
Will there still be schools to
teach subjects and fractions?

I wonder I do
What the world will be like
Will we still have cars?
Will we still have bikes?

I know very well
That I cannot tell
Because I won't be there
and I'm glad.

Michelle Ryan

The Sea

Havoc screamed at sea that night,
which left the sailors ready for
the fight of their life.

It crashed, it roared
nearly ruining the starboard
When all at once the sky cleared leaving
nothing to be feared for all was alright.

Laura Gregory

The Wind

Blow, wind blow in your wintry season,
Blow with your old wind till everything is freezing.

But in the summer you are nowhere to be found
Everything has a summery sound

Children playing having fun,
others sunbathing in the sun.

But in the spring you are a light little breeze
Fluttering along like busy little bees

And in the autumn you dance around
lifting the golden leaves from the ground.
So blow wind blow.

Pamela Maher

The School Yard

Eleven o'clock and half past twelve,
With our lunches ready to share,
Out into the school yard we scamper,
Running like mad march hares.

Howling screams from a little one,
Who fell from a bike, bought cheap,
Earrings on the older kids,
As they bound and jump and leap.

In the corner some may stand,
While teacher roams around,
Talking in whispers so she can't hear,
Not making much of a sound.

Hopscotch, skipping and chasing,
Some of the games we play,
Laughing, crying or singing,
It's fun every single day.

The babies and senior infants,
Altogether in a little clump,
While fifth and sixth sit around,
Second, third and fourth,
Play the long jump.

Different sounds, numerous games,
A happy place to be,
The playground in our school,
Drop in and you will see.

Kerri Nolan

1798

200 years today,
thousands of lives
were destroyed and taken away.

Shot, burnt and disease killed
all the lives that deserved to live.

Families torn apart
people praying they would not
take part in the crime that took
place on that very date.

So remember when you fight
just think of the people and their
pride all destroyed because of two kings.

Samantha Kenny

Babysitting

When Jamie and Ronda raced up the stairs,
the baby started crying and the cat shed hairs.
The gravy spilled over and burned our dog Rover,
there was paint in my hair and tissue everywhere.

The cups were filled with glue,
and O my gosh they're only new.
Jamie knocked Ronda's tooth out
and then she started to shout and shout.
The neighbours complained and they
will tell Mom and Dad and I'll get the blame.

Oh no it's ten to seven and
Mum and Dad will be home
with Uncle Kevin,
Oh won't he be ashamed when he sees this
mess, and we have only ten minutes or even less.

Oh no, Oh no, it's too late because
Mum and Dad's coming through the gate.

Emma Greene

Happy Day

I had a very happy day
on the very ninth of May
It was my First Communion
You see I was really shakey and
shivery,
Then my Daddy said to me
relax and take it easy.

My Dad got down on a bended knee
and said a little prayer for me.
That God's light would
shine on us
Then we went to Church and
took our place ready to receive
God's holy grace.

Then when I saw Father Farrell's smiling face
I knew for me this is the right place.

Zosia Howell

Clean Up Your Act

Clean up your act
Get down on your hands and knees,
Clean up your act,
Before you catch fleas.

Your body needs soap,
After you go to the toilet,
You must wash your hands
With Mr Soap.

Brushing your teeth is very important
You must do it at least twice a day,
And don't let those germs
get in your way.

Shaunna Wheatley

Try

When I play a football match
we try to win and to score a goal
I try to play my best
And so does the rest of the team
When I could not swim,
I kept on trying
And now I can swim
When I could not cycle my bike
I tried to but I fell off it a few times
But I tried and now I can cycle my bike

Matthew Scanlan

Witches

W — Where do they go
I — In the sky
T — Twitching witches flying up high
C — Casting spells wherever they go
H — Horrible, horrifying witches.

James McLoughlin

The Tractor

I am a tractor every morning
digging and digging in the mud.

Sometimes when I am working,
Sometimes when I am digging,
I always get stuck in the mud.

I always break down,
I always have to get repaired
When I go back to work again
I have no problems so I don't
break down again.

Gavin Kelly

The Dumpster

The Dumpster, The Dumpster,
He works all day long,
Sweeping and dusting,
Brushing and pushing.

It's not his fault,
All day at the bins,
As a matter of fact I feel sorry for him.

At the end of the day,
He gets little pay,
But he keeps our street tidy,
Let's keep it that way.

Ger Fitzgerald

The Eagle

I have pride in my eye,
I am an enemy that can fly,
I swoop down to my victim,
I crush them and pick them.

I have two golden wings,
A strong beak and things,
When my eye will glance,
My victims have no chance.

When I swoop and glide,
My victims can run but can't hide,
From the power and strength of the eagle,
I've got them from any type of angle.

When my victims come out to play,
There on a branch I'll lay,
And when my victims are about,
WATCH OUT!!!

Shane Keenan

Chewing Gum

There's ice-cream that melts on your fingers,
Lollipops that stick to your clothes,
But the one I like best is the gooey, sticky, messy
Chewing Gum that sticks anywhere.

It's orange and pink, blue and green,
yellow and brown, purple and white,
It sticks to your clothes,
It sticks to your hair,
It sticks to your fingers
and even your nose.

Mum hates it, Dad hates it,
Nan and Gran too,
But I think I quite like it,
So I'll just chew and chew.

Aisling Duffy

Terri and Geri

There was a man called Terry
Who decided to drive down to Kerry
He went in a Lada
Ended up in Nevada
Where he met a girl called Geri.

Now Geri was a spice girl
They called her Ginger spice
The others did not like her
But I thought she was nice.

Cliodhna Denny

Nag, Nag

Grown-ups nag nag nag,
and sometimes its a real drag,
Don't do this and

Don't do that
Don't bite your nails
Don't pinch the cat
If I was the boss
they'd listen to me
so I could relax and watch TV

Claire Kelly

I Wish

I wish I found
Upon the ground
A thousand pound
Then I am bound
to be very rich
And have my own
Football pitch
I'd play all day
I'd have a pool
There'd be no school
And I would rule
I wish... I wish...

Kate O'Shiel

Summer Through the Eyes of a 2 year old

Mom put this white stuff on me
It looked like squishy snow
But what it really was
I really do not know.

Mom put me in a huge bath
She said it was the sea
And what she called 'The Waves'
Kept splashing over me.

There was brown stuff on the ground
Some other children made
Big houses and big castles
With their buckets and spades.

I asked Mom why we went there
She said 'because of the sun'
I decided I want to go back there
Because I had a lot of fun

Caoimhe McCarthy

In the Morning

Come on get up
We have to go
Get out you lazy thing
Mothers throwing a boomerang
Father thinks he's a king

Lets go
The bus is on its way
Your breakfast is going cold
We have to go sometime today
God you're very bold

Screaming, shouting
There driving me crazy
I wish I could just get out of here.

I don't know what the panics about
I wish they'd all just disappear.

Briona McCarthy

Cherry Blossoms

The small pink petals of soft cherry blossoms
Scatter themselves in the breeze

Pink and white petals all over the ground
falling from pink and white trees.

They look like dancing ballerinas
When the wind blows them down

And they make such pretty patterns
When they gently touch the ground.

To stand under a blossom tree
When the wind rocks its boughs

Is a little piece of heaven
With beauty all around.

Grace O'Connor

Inside the Box You Will Find

a cute puppy jumping
a lazy lobster sleeping
a tiny ant rushing
a skinny monkey bumping
a long worm slithering
a beautiful insect running
a silly fly buzzing
inside the box
inside the box

Aoife Lennon

A New Friend

Four fat friends
Sitting under a tree
Licking their lollipops
And laughing at me

I walk past them
Feeling very sad
When people laugh at me
It makes me feel bad

I feel a touch on my shoulder
Slowly I turn around
She shook my hand
Amazed I flopped to the ground

Grace Stanley

Yellow

Yellow is the colour of the sun,
Lovely little daffodils,
Soft grainy sand,
Bitter lemons in a drink,
Cornflakes in the morning,
Cheerful swimming togs in the water,
Beautiful bouncing butterflies

Olivia Hanbidge

If I were a Princess

I would like
a huge white castle,
a tall prince with a white horse,
a waiter to give me my food,
a little brown dog,
a gold dress with glass slippers,
a black horse,
Ronan as my husband,
a rabbit with a collar,
a gold necklace,
a Boyzone tape.

Lorna Hanbidge

Love

Love is red,
It tastes like a large red apple,
Love smells like roses blooming in Spring,
It looks like swans swimming silently,
Love sounds like a baby lamb bleating,
It feels like a warm blanket wrapped around me.

Amanda Finlay

Kittens

Kind and gentle everyday
Intelligent everytime you look at them
Tempting you to do a dance
Telling you a song in kitten language
Eating lots of food everyday
Nice and cuddly for you to squeeze
Smiling at you although you don't know it

Eva Coller

Friendship

Frightened of what she'll say,
Run and hide from her,
I could say hi!,
Even say bye,
Never will I talk,
Don't know what to say,
She's all alone,
Hate to say hello,
I hope she likes me,
Petrified I said Hi!

Sheree Moody

Spider

Spin spider spin
Pounce on your prey
Inside the house there is a man
Duck spider duck
Eat your prey
Run away

Edwina Hanbidge

Hedgehog

Hedgehog you are so spiky
That's why I like you
Hope you don't die
Or else I'll cry
I shall bury you with leaves

Sharleen Moody

The Poor

When I see a drop of rain
I think, thank God I'm not in pain
The number of kids that die each year
And here we are thinking of our career
While they starve and thirst and live in fear

I look close into that drop of rain
But really it's still insane
They have no rain
They have no WATER!
And we sit here and stuff ourselves
While they sit there with empty shelves.

So help a bit, just give a little
We're not dying our bones aren't brittle
So give your amount and it will count
For the poor people of the world.

Aisling Murray

A Witch Recipe

Gather together for this wonderful stew,
A toad's wart of any sort,
Mix in a bat's wing,
Not forgetting dead wasp's sting,
A mole's nose would give it a zing,
Then add a green toe,
Tongue of a dog,
Eye of a hog,
Of course a frog's leg,
A blind mouse's ear,
A finger from any old fellow,
Mix until yellow,
In a cauldron,
Burning hot,
Serve on a monster's spit,
And what have you got?
A most wonderful witches stew.

Katie Evans

A Bad School Day

Every morning I get up at eight,
Mum shouts 'Hurry or you'll be late',
I eat my brekky as fast as I can,
I look at the clock and I cry 'Oh Man!'
Into the car and off we go,
Then I shout, Mum — you're going too slow!

At last I got into the room,
Teacher was cross and full of gloom,
I said to myself, 'Mum, I'll kill you so,'
Then I just remembered, she's not here, Oh blow!
I sat in my seat feeling really bad,
but then Teacher said, 'Not much homework,'
I felt quite glad ...
After the day I was worn out...
then there was my diary — which, of course,
I had forgotten all about.

Laura Demery

An Excuse and Exaggeration

I was swimming in the lake,
When I saw the whole place shake,
And a whale came up and saw me,
Eating chocolate cake,
He licked his lips and giggled,
As I began to shiver,
And all in one gulp,
It was stuck in a sulk,
In a dark gloomy stomach,
In there I met a deaf fat man,
He was driving an ice-cream van,
I asked him did he have a feather,
He replied 'here's some heather,'
I said to him that will do,
I tickled the whale until he said 'atishoo',
Then I had to swim back to shore,
And my back is quite sore,
Really it wasn't fun,
That is why my homework is not done.

Grainne Earley

Kittens

Late one night,
Out of sight,
The mum gave birth to four
Kittens by the door.

There was a black and white,
Who was as black as night,
And as white as snow,
With a button nose.

There were two tabby greys,
Who stayed with their mother for days,
But after that the girl was quiet,
And the boy became a riot.

And last but not least was a black one,
Who is very cute and a lot of fun,
But as he gets older,
He's getting bolder.

Alison Dunne

Witches Recipe

Starters:
Well we have a cup of sick two dog's legs
and two frog's heads, a gut from a pig and
a big tooth from a crock.

Dinner:
A glass of spit and a kitten's nose, a big
heart from a bear, a big tummy of a human
being which witches eat as beans.

Dessert:
An ice cube with baby spiders in it,
a drink of rotten apple mashed and some ants,
a heart bobbling in the pot (makes a juicy strawberry).

Caoilfhionn Deeney

War and Peace

War is such a terrible thing,
Aren't they every going to stop,
Really they are acting like two-year olds.

Armies of soldiers everywhere,
Never stopping to think about whom they are killing,
Doing what they themselves think is right.

Please let them stop the killing,
Even of innocent children,
And let the victims rest in peace,
Call a stop to all the fighting,
Everyone should live in peace.

Anna B. Ruth

January

January is a moody month,
It never makes up its mind,
Between glorious days and freezing days,
I never know which to expect,
It's supposed to welcome the New Year,
Though this year I'm not sure it did,
With storms here and there,
And no electricity through the night,
The New Year was spent without any light.

But last year the weather wasn't stormy,
And we celebrated right through the night,
And when we woke up on New Year's Day,
The first day of January was delight.

Chloe Kinsella

The Prayer of the Crocus

Lord I am the crocus
I just want to say
thank you for rain
sun and for my other friends
the tulips the daffodils and
the hyacinths
If it was not for the rain and the sun
I would not be alive
this very day now I may say
Amen

Sally O'Neill

Tennis

Bounce hit, bounce hit,
That's the way you play it
Keep the ball over the net
Try and win every set

Serve and rally
Slice and volley
Forehand and backhand
It's a competitive hobby

Arantxa and Henman
They're the best
Playing in Wimbledon
They beat all the rest

My partner and I
We don't win much
It's a lot of fun
We just need the right touch

Keeping score
That's the catch
Deuce and van
Game, Set and Match

Karen McArdle

Dad's Breakfast

Oh no Dad is doing breakfast
His eggs are as flat as a pancake
His sausages are as fat as butter
His bacon is as black as coal
His tea is as hot as a furnace that
burns your mouth off,
Oh Dad's at work, Thank God!

Niamh Dolan

A Bowl of Fruit

I sit on the table day out and day in,
Just silent and waiting, never making a din.
I've oranges and apples and bananas too,
Won't somebody take one, Well, how about you?

Dad comes in and passes me by,
Johnny and his friends but they're all too shy,
Mommy's too busy, never takes a break,
If she does, she'll have tea or coffee and cake.

At Hallowe'en I'm overflowing,
Adults and children keep coming and going,
But the rest of the year I just sit and I wait,
For someone to choose a mango or date.

Paula Byrne

Mixed Feelings

My little raft is like my ship,
That sails across the sea.
At night the trees are monsters,
Out to get me.

The grass grows long,
Like the summer days,
Lawnmowers are cows,
That constantly graze.

Sarah Ryan

Summertime

Summertime is full of joy,
Happiness and fun,
So put on your shorts,
Slap on the cream,
And sunbathe in front of the sun.

Some people go on holidays,
To France, Greece or Spain,
In these places the sunshine glares,
And sunburn can be a pain.

But if you are staying at home,
Where the sunshine isn't so great,
Go out with your friends and enjoy yourself,
But don't stay out too late.

Julie Traynor

One to Ten

One wounded wallaby waddled on a walkway
Two talking telephones talked in a taxi
Three thorny things thought up a theory
Four fat frogs flirted furiously
Five fair flies founded France
Six slimy slugs slithered steadily
Seven sly snobs sold a settee
Eight evicted natives narrated the news
Ten terrible teachers taught terrible things.

Fiona Whelan

Cheetah

A cheetah is fast
He never comes last
He always gets his prey
The proper way
He brings home his food
But when eating can be rude

John Hanbidge

The Pea

I went into a house to see
A man eating a single pea
He cut, he ate, he munched and chopped,
But off his plate the pea popped.

It rolled across the floor
and through the crack under the door,
It rolled into the garden
and bounced down the steps.

It wandered round the garden
and under the hedge
There it stayed and didn't move
It lodged itself in a grove.

A year or so later,
the man looked out of his window to see
A bush that had grown
from the troublesome pea.

Anne Marie Griffin